SHARK SHARK ATTACK!

Discovery CHANNEL

TOP 10 ATTACK SHARKS

Written by **Mark Shulman**
Designed by **On-Purpos, Inc.**

Contributing consultant: **Sylvia M. James,**
former Director of Education of the
National Aquarium in Baltimore

Meredith Books
Des Moines, Iowa

Jane Root, Executive Vice President & General Manager, Discovery Channel
Carol LeBlanc, Vice President, Licensing
Elizabeth Bakacs, Vice President, Creative Services
Maren Herzog, Manager, Creative Services
Caitlin Erb, Licensing Specialist

www.discovery.com

Meredith Books
1716 Locust St.
Des Moines, IA 50309-3023
meredithbooks.com

First Edition.

Manufactured and printed in China.
ISBN 978-0-696-23692-1 (perfect bound)
ISBN 978-0-696-23278-7 (saddle stitch)

© **Gary Bell**/oceanwideimages.com, Great White shark, cover; Tiger shark, pages 34, 47.
Georgette Douwma, photographer, Whale shark and scuba divers, pages 14, 15.
© **Chris & Monique Fallows**/oceanwideimages.com, Shortfin Mako shark, page 26; Bull shark, pages 32, 47.
© **Andy Murch**/oceanwideimages.com, Lemon shark, page 18.
Carl Roessler, photographer, Silvertip shark in a classic sweep, pages 6, 7, 9; Great White shark, pages 16, 17, 36, 37, 42, 45, 46, 47, back cover; Hammerhead shark, pages 22, 23, close up of head of Great white shark, page 41.
© **Jeffrey L. Rotman**/CORBIS, Mouth of Caribbean reef shark, page 9; Sand tiger shark (Eugomphodus taurus), jaws open, underwater view. Other common names: grey nurse shark, spotted ragged tooth. Sand tiger sharks are found in shallow bays, coastal waters and reef areas in the western and eastern Atlantic, western Indian Ocean and western Pacific, pages 9, 11; Basking shark feeding on plankton, pages 7, 15, back cover.

CONTENTS

HELP! SHARK!

They strike without warning. They strike fear in your heart. They patrol the waters silently, swiftly, relentlessly. They are fascinating animals.

No other creature is so feared and so misunderstood.

Before dinosaurs there were sharks, and they've terrorized the seas for 400 million years. What is the deep, dark secret of their success? Unlike dinosaurs, sharks survived all the ice ages underwater, unaffected by global cooling. During that time, these apex predators honed their skills to become incredibly efficient killing machines—with the jaws, the teeth, and the killer instinct to stay at the top of the food chain.

Inside *Shark Attack*, you'll encounter the largest, the fastest, and the most deadly fish in the sea. You'll meet the meals as well as the marauders. You'll find which 10 sharks are the deadliest to humans. It's an open and shut case.

COME ON, DIVE IN TO SHARK ATTACK. WHAT ARE YOU AFRAID OF?

SHARK B

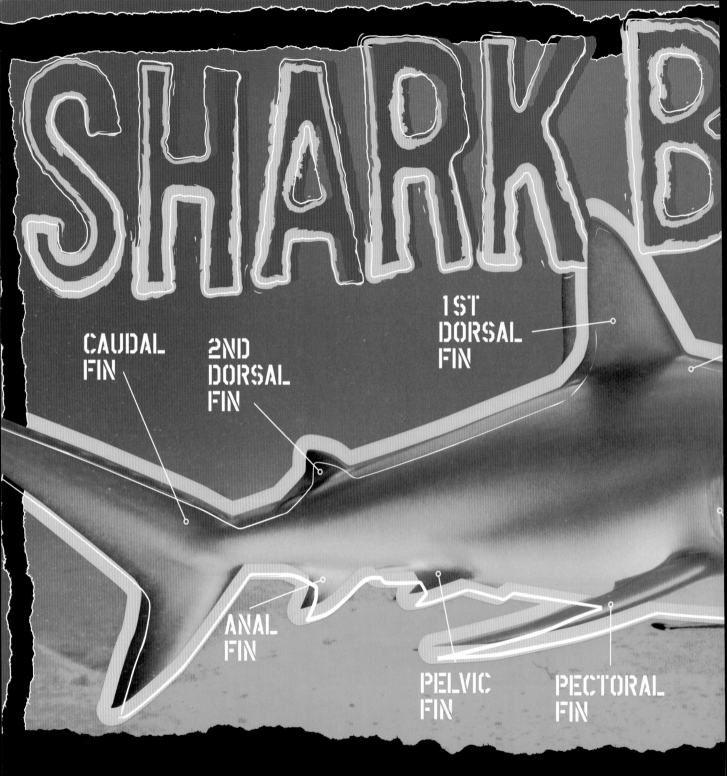

CAUDAL
FIN

2ND
DORSAL
FIN

1ST
DORSAL
FIN

ANAL
FIN

PELVIC
FIN

PECTORAL
FIN

FILTERING GILLS

Like other fish a shark breathes through gills. The six or so pairs of gills filter the oxygen from the surrounding water. Sharks constantly need water flowing through the gills in order to breathe. In most species, water moves over the gills when the shark swims.

DORSAL FIN

The dorsal fin, located on a shark's back (the upper side of its body), helps the shark keep its balance. So does the pelvic fin down under. As moviemakers know, a dorsal fin looks cool popping out of the water—unless it's headed in your direction.

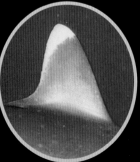

BASICS

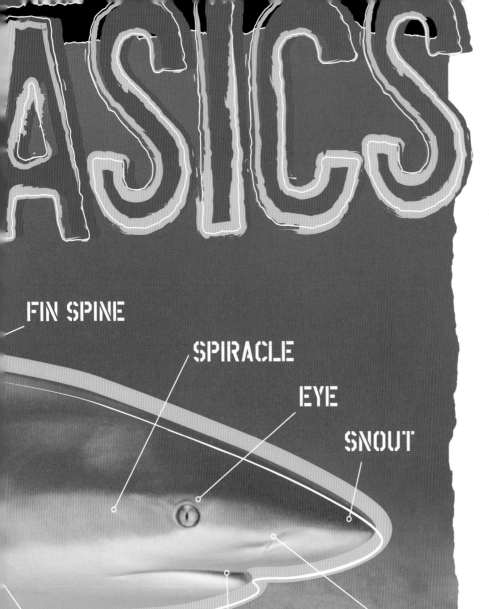

- FIN SPINE
- SPIRACLE
- EYE
- SNOUT
- NOSTRIL
- GILL SLITS
- MOUTH

MIRACLE SPIRACLES

Certain sharks, such as the nurse shark, need extra help getting water to their gills. For them, spiracles are miracles of nature. These openings are located behind the eyes and help those particular sharks breathe when they're eating or resting.

BRAINS

A shark's brain is large for its body, more like a mammal's than a fish's. Two-thirds of a shark's brain is dedicated to smell.

LIVER LOVERS

Why can't sharks stop swimming? Because if they do stop swimming, they'll sink. Unlike other fish, sharks don't have a bladder filled with gas to help them float. The shark's oil-filled liver is what keeps it buoyant. No wonder the liver makes up 15 to 25 percent of a shark's total weight.

SUPPLE SKELETON

Sharks have no bones. Surprised? What holds them together is actually cartilage, the same stuff that holds your nose together. Having a cartilage skeleton is very useful—sharks are more flexible than boned animals. They can attack more forcefully and slip away easily.

A STRANGE TONGUE

A shark's tongue is called a basihyal and it doesn't move. Therefore it really doesn't do much. It's made of cartilage and is grayish or white in color.

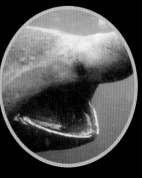

SHARK SENSE

Nature really seems to love the shark. As if they weren't already perfect killing machines, sharks have an unmatched ability to sense—without seeing, smelling, or hearing—the presence of a future victim.

As it so happens every living animal on Earth generates an electrical field. And it also happens that sharks can locate these electrical fields the way you can locate the direction of a police siren. Their receptors, the ampullae of Lorenzini, are found near the shark's eyes, snout, and mouth, and they can pick up the incredibly low levels of electrical energy that turtles and swordfish emit. Scientists believe that sharks also use these receptors to navigate by following the planet's natural magnetic fields.

FEELING:

Sharks do have feelings, but not like humans. Sharks are able to detect motion through water movement, using lateral lines that are on both sides of their body, running from its head to its tail. Through the use of the lateral line, sharks can detect erratic motions that are 3 to 10 feet away. Sharks also detect prey by bumping into it.

SEEING:

Sharks have excellent vision that is especially suited for the darkness of the sea. In fact they can see in one-tenth of the light that humans need. Sharks can make out different colors and their only shortcoming when it comes to vision is that close-up objects get blurry. Maybe that's why they sometimes mistake people for dolphins. Maximum sight distance: about 50 feet.

SMELLING:

Don't even try to compare your nose with a shark's precision equipment. Sharks can smell a few drops of blood a mile away. They can smell the oil of small fish from almost as far. A shark has a nasal cavity on the left and right sides of its nose that helps detect which direction the scent is coming from. Maximum smelling distance: 1 mile.

HEARING:

Sharks can hear very well. They can detect low frequencies that humans can't hear, but humans can pick up higher frequencies than they can, so it's a wash. Maximum hearing distance: about 2-3 miles.

TASTING:

Sharks prefer fatty, easy-to-swallow victims, especially the kind that don't bite back. Sharks have taste buds in their mouths and throats, not on their tongues like humans. If a shark doesn't like what it tastes, it will spit it out. Scientists believe humans just don't taste good to sharks.

SHARK

There is no animal on Earth with more biting force than a shark. Sharks are nature's ultimate biting machines. What helps a shark leave such a mark? Almost every animal—including you—has a lower jaw that is hinged into the skull. Not the mighty sharks. They have upper and lower jaws, and each one moves independently. Here's how. (Warning: If you're squeamish, stop reading here and jump to the next paragraph.) A shark bites first with its lower jaw. Then the upper jaw takes a chomp. The shark tears away at its dinner by moving its head back and forth, taking several bites from its prey. The chunks of meat are not chewed up as you might guess. Instead they are swallowed whole in big gulps. You would think with all the teeth they have, sharks would chew their food more.

CHEW ON THIS
Sharks have several hundred teeth in their jaws at any time. Some have as many as 3,000 teeth at once. These teeth are set back in rows; some sharks have 15 or more rows of teeth in each jaw, but the average is about five rows.

The teeth of the carnivorous sharks don't stick around for long. On the smaller sharks they last about 10 days. On the larger ones they can last up to six months. These teeth usually fall out after an attack. Why? The teeth of sharks don't have roots to keep them in; they're only held by soft tissue. One bite and that tooth is swimming away. After a shark's tooth comes out, a new one moves into its place from the row behind in a day or two. And best yet, the new tooth is generally larger than the one it replaces.

QUANTITY, NOT QUALITY
Some species of sharks lose and replace between 20,000 and 30,000 teeth in their lifetimes. Imagine if they received a dollar from the tooth fairy for every tooth!

IT'S WIDE INSIDE
The shark's jaws are not permanently connected to its skull the way yours are. This handy feature helps a shark "dislocate" its jaws, make a wider gape, and get large prey into its mouth.

BITES

A WHALE OF A BITE

A giant among sharks, the whale shark has up to 300 rows of teeth. These rows of teeth (some as small as yours) aren't used for biting. Instead these little nubbins help filter the delicious shrimp, plankton, and other minimeals that whale sharks eat by the millions.

GET THE POINT

Different sharks have different shape teeth. Some sharks, such as the great white, have jagged teeth like the ones on saw blades. Others, such as the sand tiger shark, have long, narrow teeth. On all sharks the front teeth are the largest and sharpest because they have the hardest work to do. Sharks don't have grinding teeth (like molars), which explains their tear-and-gulp diet. When a front tooth breaks off, the back tooth that's preparing to move into the lost tooth's place gets honed for action. The replacement tooth moves forward and a new tooth forms in its place. Sharks' teeth are like a paddle wheel—as one falls out, another takes its place. Isn't that sharp?

Almost every species of shark has a different appetite and not all sharks attack and eat large prey. Shark diets can include anything from tiny plankton, crabs, and lobsters to larger fish and sea mammals. Great whites can eat hundreds of pounds at a time. The scavenger tiger sharks take dinner dead or alive, eating anything they find, including tires, gasoline cans, and license plates. The enormous whale shark uses its 4-foot-wide jaws and 300 rows of teeth to swallow a galaxy of microscopic plankton and about 1,500 gallons of seawater per hour.

Although some have giant appetites, most sharks eat just 2 percent of their body weight per day. If you weigh 100 pounds and eat 2 pounds of food daily (a 1-pound steak dinner with potatoes and salad would do it) you'd be on par. Except for a few gluttons, sharks are average eaters with big reputations. Being cold-blooded also means they don't eat as much as warm-blooded humans.

A variety of sharks can go days, weeks, or even months between meals. One sand tiger shark in captivity reportedly went 15 months without eating. How do they do it? They store oil in their livers. Oil makes a handy portable meal in the cold and dark—but it can't be as tasty as the following fellows on the next page.

SEABIRDS

One moment they're floating along, happily bobbing on the waves. The next moment, snap!

PLANKTON, BRINE SHRIMP, ETC.

Don't laugh. These tiny creatures feed the world's largest fish. Whale sharks eat millions a day.

BITS OF WHALES

The cookie-cutter shark, small but brave, will sidle up to a whale and chomp off a bite. Guess how it got its name?

FELLOW SHARKS

Sharks aren't proud. They have good taste. And they taste good. Shark cannibalism keeps it in the family.

FLOATING TRASH

Sharks aren't big chewers. They like to swallow something whole. No wonder tiger sharks and some other large species can swallow whatever people pollute their ocean home with.

SEALS AND SEA LIONS

An excellent source of tasty fat to keep sharks warm and cozy.

RAYS

A challenge to chase and eat, rays fight back. Strictly for the larger sharks.

FISH, FISH, FISH

What else would you expect a carnivore to find in the ocean?

SHELLFISH

You can't afford clams and lobsters every night, but sharks find all they can eat.

TURTLES

More nutritious than you might think. And very easy to catch. Crunchy too.

AND . . .

No, sharks don't normally eat people. A few bite, and you could be attacked if you happen to smell like blood or other things delicious to a shark. If you think your chance of being shark bait is great . . . you're out to lunch!

SHARK E

THE LARGEST

At sizes up to 50 feet long, the whale shark is the world's largest shark. It's also the world's largest fish and has the largest mouth of any fish (up to 4 feet wide).

Interestingly the peaceful whale shark primarily eats tiny plankton—and lots of it—by opening its mouth and letting the plankton filter through as it swims. Imagine walking into a swarm of mosquitoes with your mouth open. Mmm, yeah!

THE SMALLEST

Look closely for three little species, the spined pygmy shark, the dwarf dogshark, and the dwarf lanternshark. Each of them grows (if that's what you call it) to about 6 to 8 inches as adults. Don't worry—your toes are safe. There are no recorded attacks on humans—yet.

TREMES

THE OLDEST
The extinct Megalodon (known only from fossils) was a large shark, maybe the largest sea creature ever. Most recent fossil specimen dates from about 25 million years ago. These behemoths grew up to 60 feet long. That's longer than a school bus! All that's left are their massive jaws with 6- to 8-inch teeth. Aren't you glad you were born after they went extinct?

LONGEST LIVING SHARK
The spiny dogfish shark has a life expectancy of between 70 and 100 years. Just like you!

DEEPEST-DIVING SHARK
The Portuguese shark has been discovered at depths below 8,900 feet. That's nearly 1.7 miles down.

FARTHEST
A blue shark was captured in Brazil, 16 months after having been tagged near New York. The shortest distance between those two points is at least 3,800 miles.

ONGEST BIT
ard for strongest shark s given to a dusky shark, jaws—according to ements—exerted a deadly unds of force.

FASTEST
Nobody how fast the fastest shark ut everyone agrees the nner for speed is the mako Some sources say the mako en clocked at 23 mph. say they've cruised ph. Either way nt to be out of the n average shark's s just 2 to 3 mph, r information.

THE 2ND LARGEST
The second largest shark is the basking shark, which is another big eater of little critters. Basking sharks can grow to be about 33 feet long.

15

The top 10 attack sharks earned their ranking based on provoked and unprovoked attacks on humans and boats. However some sharks are difficult to identify, especially during an attack situation, which can skew the data toward more identifiable sharks, such as great white, tiger, hammerhead, and nurse sharks.

The top 3 attack sharks earned their reputation because they are aggressive and dangerous, not to mention they live in widespread areas. Each one is at least 7 feet long and to them, humans appear as prey, which is often fatal because their first bite is so powerful.

However there are fewer than 100 shark attacks a year, and fewer than 10 percent of these are fatal. When you consider the number of people swimming, surfing, diving, or just spending time in the oceans, this number is exceptionally low.

LEMON

(Negaprion brevirostris)

Lemon sharks have long, thin, sharp teeth—the kind that are perfect for catching slippery fish. They also eat rays, crustaceans, sea birds, and smaller sharks. They have the ability to hang out without moving on sandy and muddy bottoms, which helps them capture their prey. The lemon shark does not gorge; it only eats until it's full and then waits for its food to be digested before eating again.

SWIMMING WITH THE SHARKS

Lemon sharks can swim .3 to .4 body lengths per second. If you do the math, you'll discover that a lemon shark can swim the distance equivalent to its body length in 2.5 to 3 seconds. In the time it takes you to read this sentence, the lemon shark has swum 15 feet. Lemon sharks actually like the company of other lemon sharks and sometimes travel in groups.

HUMAN ATTACK RANKING #10

OTHER NAMES? In France, it's known as requin citron and in the Netherlands it's citroenhaii.

HOW LONG? 8 to 10 feet

HOW HEAVY? 200 pounds

HOW FAST? Up to 20 mph

LEMON FRESH? No, they don't like fresh water.

SHARK

THE BIGGEST

The lemon shark is one of the larger species of sharks. The largest one ever recorded was 13 feet in length.

LITTLE LEMONS

Young lemon sharks lose an entire set of teeth, one at a time, every seven to eight days. As their teeth are coming out, new teeth are quickly coming in at the back of their jaw. These teeth then rotate to the front.

HOW THEY ATTACK

Lemon sharks are shy and tend to avoid confrontation with humans unless provoked. However, when their space is invaded, they become aggressive. That said, this could be due to the fact that the lemon shark is nocturnal—swimming and eating at night. None of the reported lemon shark attacks have been fatal.

MELLOW YELLOW

The lemon shark is named for its coloring, which is deep yellow like the fruit. Its belly is off-white.

BLUE SH

(Prionace glauca)

HUMAN ATTACK RANKING

#9

NICKNAMES? Blue Dog, Blue Whaler

HOW LONG? 6 to 12.5 feet

HOW HEAVY? 260 to 400 pounds

IF ATTACKED? It's you who'll be blue.

THE BIGGEST? The largest verified blue shark was 12.5 feet long and weighed 490 pounds.

BLUES CRUISE

Blue sharks do things in a big way. They're among the fastest sharks in the water and have been clocked at more than 20 mph. They like to travel long distances, routinely taking journeys of over a thousand miles. Speedy, spread out, and prolific, this species is one of the most abundant sharks in the world's waters. Their long, slender bodies make them agile in the water, and their extra-long tail fins make them powerful swimmers. They have bright blue skin, with white underbellies. Their schools are often divided by size and gender.

B lue sharks have made the North Atlantic their superhighway. This high-speed shark has been regularly tracked on journeys of 1,200 to 1,700 miles, and one blue that was studied swam more than 3,700 miles between New York and Brazil.

BLUE SHARKS:

▸ in the Pacific Ocean can be 25 percent smaller than their Atlantic Ocean siblings
▸ are social fish: blues often congregate in large groups
▸ chew like champs with pointed, serrated saw-blade teeth

HOW THEY ATTACK

The blue shark is ranked as one of the top 10 deadliest sharks because it is often the first responder to air and sea disasters. When people aren't dropping in for dinner, the blue has a proven method for scoring a fresh catch. It just opens its mouth and charges straight through a school of fish, a pod of dolphins, a turn of turtles, or even an ugly of walruses. (These are all actual terms for these groups of animals.) A blue sways its head from side to side to increase its odds of finding a tasty bite. The blue has been known to circle its prey before attacking.

HAMMER

(Sphyrna mokarran)

HUMAN ATTACK RANKING #8

NICKNAMES? It doesn't need nicknames.

HOW LONG? 6 to 10 feet

HOW HEAVY? 100 to 350 pounds

CAN IT HAMMER NAILS? No, but it might nail you.

HEAD

HOW THEY ATTACK
When it's on the hunt—which is often for this is a large, hungry animal—the great hammerhead glides over sand and reefs, back and forth, in shallower waters. It swings its huge head with a dramatic sway so it can see what, or who, is up ahead. This shark can become very bold, swinging close to divers and surfers but rarely attacking. If they (the sharks) feel threatened however, the people they encounter may be in for trouble.

THE BIGGEST
The greatest great hammerheads have grown to 20 feet long and weighed more than 1,000 pounds.

TERRIBLE TEETH
Their triangular teeth are as sharp and serrated as saw blades, which could widen your eyes as well.

D on't let its good looks fool you—the great hammerhead is one of the fiercest predatory sharks in the sea. And it has a famous appetite. Though similar to its kinder, gentler hammerhead cousins, the great hammerhead has racked up a significant history of human attacks. It has a wide, thick head like a steel beam, with probing eyes at the far ends. This arrangement gives hammerheads the best possible peripheral vision. A bumpy nose completes the hammer image. The great hammerhead has a gray-brown body, a light underbelly, and a large, tapered dorsal fin.

NO STING
This predator likes to pin stingrays to the sand with its trademark hammer-shaped head. Let the stingray sting all it likes before it's eaten—hammerheads have a built-in defense against the sting.

GREAT HAMMERHEADS:
▸ are cannibals who happily hunt their fellow sharks
▸ are a regular meal, when young, for other species of sharks

BLACKT[

(Carcharhinus limbatus)

HUMAN ATTACK RANKING

#7

NICKNAMES? Spot-fin Ground Shark

HOW LONG? 4 to 6 feet

HOW HEAVY? 35 to 60 pounds

IF YOU SPOT THE SPOT-FIN? Swim toward shore!

PSHARK

THE BIGGEST

The largest reported blacktip shark measured in at a long, lean 8.5 feet and weighed only 84 pounds.

AUMAKUA

Some native Hawaiians believe the blacktip is lucky. They call it aumakua, which means guardian spirit. Hawaii is one place where the sharks aren't hunted or eaten; instead they're given food and good wishes.

The distinctive blacktip shark may be small, but it leaves a big impression—mainly on people's legs and arms. What puts this little biter so high on the shark attack list? Many of its recorded attacks against humans have led to fatalities. Some experts believe that the easy-to-spot blacktip is getting too much credit for what other sharks do. Blacktips have full bodies, long snouts, and gray skin. Check out that high dorsal fin if you want to see how the blacktip got its name: A signature spot of black on the top fin makes for an impressive entrance.

HOW THEY ATTACK

They pause, they spring, they lunge at a school of fish from below, and they don't stop until they've broken the surface. Then the blacktip leaps out and does a 360-degree barrel roll (or two). See spot jump! Blacktips seem to be especially fond of attacking surfers, maybe because surfers also jump and spin above the waves. Though the blacktip is a worldwide wanderer, a great number of blacktip attacks are reported in U.S. waters.

BLACKTIP SHARKS:

- are killed in the millions each year by humans for food and leather
- are often eaten by far larger tiger sharks when they are young
- get credited with one-sixth of all shark attacks in Florida

SHORTFIN

(Isurus oxyrinchus)

#6

NICKNAMES? Blue Pointer, Blue Dynamite

HOW LONG? 6 to 13 feet

HOW HEAVY? 135 to 300 pounds

GOING FISHING? Make sure it's not fishing for you.

MAKO

The shortfin mako is one of the fastest sharks in the ocean and one of the most fearless attackers. These metallic blue rockets are known to reach swimming speeds of 22 mph, which is up to seven times faster than some of their shark cousins. You say speed isn't everything? You're right. The mako can also leap higher than nearly any other fish: 15 to 20 feet high. They usually take three leaps at a time, and it's the third one that's the highest. These slender shooting stars have long, pointed snouts and big black eyes. It all adds up to make them one of the most prized trophy catches of sport fishing.

THE BIGGEST
The largest verified shortfin mako ever caught was a female that was 13 feet long and weighed 1,115 pounds. Not so short after all.

FAST FINS OR FISH TALES?
Some witnesses say they've seen the mako approach speeds up to 60 mph. Who knows?

HOW THEY ATTACK
The shortfin mako seems to have no fear. Divers who come close are greeted with threatening advances that signal an imminent attack. It approaches with its mouth open and swims around its prey in a figure eight. Humans who try to hook them or hassle them find a fast, aggressive, angry shark on their hands. Shortfins like to turn on their human predators by attacking, smashing, and jumping into the fishing boats that stalk them.

THE NAME
The term mako comes from a native New Zealand Maori word meaning "blue lightning." They should know—their islands are surrounded with these shocking sharks.

SHORTFIN MAKO SHARKS:

▸ can swim up to 40 miles in a day and more than 1,000 miles on long-distance journeys
▸ have terrible triangular teeth that show even when their mouths are closed
▸ mainly eat bony fish and also enjoy porpoises, turtles, and other sharks
▸ are second only to great whites when it comes to attacks on boats

NURSE

(Ginglymostoma cirratum)

HUMAN ATTACK RANKING

#5

NICKNAME? Cat Shark

HOW LONG? 7 to 14 feet

HOW HEAVY? 160 to 280 pounds

WHY CALLED NURSE SHARK? You might need one.

SHARK

They may be called nurse sharks, but like every other shark they only take care of themselves. By day the sluggish nurse shark rests at the bottom of the sea. At night they get active and the real feeding begins. Nurse sharks spend most of their time as bottom dwellers, and they have the looks to prove it. Their distinctive, vacuum cleaner faces are ideally suited for sucking tasty shellfish and other unlucky creatures off the seafloor. Nurse sharks are brownish, often covered with spots, and have big, rounded dorsal fins. They have exceptionally strong jaws, even for a shark.

THE BIGGEST
The largest nurse shark on record was 11.5 feet long and weighed 365 pounds.

NURSING SCHOOLS
During their daily downtime nurse sharks are social animals. They rest in schools of 30 or more, waiting for night to come. When it does and the prowling starts, they become solitary supper searchers.

AMBUSH
How do they get dinner while sitting still at the bottom of the sea? Younger nurses seem to sleep while resting on their bellies with their snouts pointed upward. Some people believe they're setting a trap for shellfish to drift beneath their snouts and get trapped.

NURSING HOME
Nurse sharks have a domestic side too. Usually they pick a cave or somewhere under a ledge to call home and return there every day at resting time.

HOW THEY ATTACK
Nurse sharks are not naturally looking for a fight, at least not with humans. They'd rather swim away than take a bite. But don't provoke one either. They don't like intruders and will defend their territory. These "cat sharks" don't pussyfoot around: They'll charge head-on and sink their teeth into interlopers. They can cause significant injury and won't always let go. Sometimes special, heavy-duty equipment is needed to pry their jaws apart.

NURSE SHARKS:
▶ are able to keep still, unlike most sharks that have to keep moving
▶ trap shellfish by remaining perfectly still and posing as rock shelters
▶ are edible, but are mostly prized for their leathery skin
▶ can suck in their prey with a powerful natural suction

SAND TIGER

(Carcharius taurus)

When you think "scary sharks," you're probably imagining the sand tiger. With its long, flat snout, wide-open mouth, and jagged teeth jutting out, it's the very picture of peril. And it has two large dorsal fins that seem to spell double trouble. But looks are somewhat deceiving—these sharks are usually shy. They have brownish gray skin and dark spots, with an off-white belly. Sand tigers often hide or sleep in caves and other snug places by day, coming out at night to feed. They are also more social than other sharks—they often travel and hunt together.

HUMAN ATTACK RANKING

#4

NICKNAMES? The Grey Nurse, Spotted Ragged-Tooth

HOW LONG? 4 to 10 feet

HOW HEAVY? 200 to 300 pounds

WHY IS IT NICKNAMED "RAGGED-TOOTH"? You don't want to find out.

R SHARK

HOW THEY ATTACK

Though it's usually a slow mover, this large ocean predator can be dangerous to swimmers. And it's one strong swimmer itself, able to lunge forward with great speed. Sand tigers will watch you with their catlike eyes and float motionless, thanks to their ability to hold big gulps of air. Usually they'll leave you alone unless you approach too closely. Then it's anybody's guess what happens next.

THE BIGGEST

The largest sand tigers have reached 11 feet long and weighed more than 700 pounds.

SAND TIGERS:

- ▶ eat mainly fish and eels
- ▶ are more social than most sharks
- ▶ do most of their prowling at night
- ▶ migrate 2,000 miles or more every year

SEE FOR YOURSELF

Why are sand tigers among the most common sharks at aquariums? Their fierce, open mouths and saw-blade teeth make quite a show. They can also live longer in captivity than most sharks—up to 10 years.

BULL SH

(Carcharhinus leucas)

NICKNAMES? Shovelnose Shark, River Shark, Freshwater Whaler

HOW LONG? 7 to 10 feet

HOW HEAVY? 200 to more than 400 pounds

LARGER THAN A REAL BULL? Sometimes longer, but not heavie

SHARK

GO JUMP IN A LAKE

How did bull sharks get into lakes such as Lake Nicaragua in Central America, whose tributaries flow out of the lakes? Bulls can jump upstream in the feeder rivers, swimming against the rapids just like one of their favorite meals: the salmon.

BULLDOZERS

Bull sharks act slow and sluggish, but when it's time to attack, they're as powerful as bulls. When they're not on a rampage, they go no faster than 3 mph. When there's dinner afloat, however, they can bust a 20 mph move.

WHEN THEY ATTACK

Bulls like the blitz assault best. The element of surprise works in their favor when the water is murky and shallow. First they give their potential victims a high-speed shove with their snout. With their prey off guard, the bull strikes again for the kill. Razor-sharp teeth, which are an inch long, are a tremendous help. If one comes out, another grows right back. This is no picky eater either. Bull sharks are known to down whatever is swimming nearby. If something swims, they'll try to swallow it.

ON THE MOVE

Annual migrations of more than 2,000 miles are common. But bull sharks rarely head far from land.

ull sharks are deadly because they can get to places where people swim. They can also prowl in freshwater or salt water. Bulls may be smaller than the great white and the tiger shark, and they may seem docile—but they can become fast and aggressive. They are more likely to provoke an attack than their larger cousins.

Adult males can grow to 7 feet long and weigh 200 pounds. And the males look like guppies next to their mates: Adult females sometimes grow to 10 feet long, weighing more than 400 pounds. Bulls have gray bodies with white underbellies. Their eyes and noses are small. But their appetites are not.

THE BIGGEST

The largest bull shark on record was nearly 12 feet long and weighed more than 500 pounds.

GETTING FRESH

The bull is one of very few sharks that can live in salt water and freshwater. When it goes into freshwater rivers, it releases salt. When it goes back to the sea, it retains more. This special skill gives the bull shark plenty of places to find prey.

RIVER WATCH

Bulls like rivers. The Amazon and the mighty Mississippi are home to the bull shark. Kayak with care!

NAME THAT NOSE

The bull shark's snout is wide and flat. Some say it looks like a bull, and others say it looks like a shovel. That's why this ferocious fish is also called the shovelnose shark. Some even call it the square-nose shark. But bull sharks don't care about their looks: They have poor eyesight.

TIGER SH

(Galeocerdo cuvier)

HUMAN ATTACK RANKING

#2

NICKNAMES? Leopard Shark, Man-eater Shark

HOW LONG? 10 to 18 feet

HOW HEAVY? 2,000 pounds and more

ACTUAL RELATION TO TIGER? Extremely distant

ARK

The tiger shark is one of the world's largest sharks. It's also one of the deadliest. There are even sailors who would prefer their odds with a great white over a "terrible tiger."

After the great white, tiger sharks have more human kills to their credit than any shark. Tiger sharks may not be as big as great whites, but averaging 15 to 20 feet long, they're one of the largest shark species. Tigers get their name from the darkish stripes on their backs. These stripes fade as they get older, but their hunger doesn't fade one bit.

CANNIBALS AND CAN OPENERS

Tiger sharks are scavengers, which means they're not picky if their "catch" is already dead. Tigers will happily eat other sharks. They'll also eat cans, license plates, and other junk thrown overboard. And they never tire of tires. It's no surprise tigers have been called "garbage can sharks."

BIG MOUTHS

The jaws of the tiger shark are massive. The jaws of some specimen skeletons are more than 2 feet wide and almost 2 feet high. Most kids could fit through the hole between the toothy upper and lower jaws. By the way, the teeth are razor sharp with jagged saw-blade edges. Ouch.

PREDATOR POWER

Tiger sharks are usually slow movers—averaging just 2 or 3 mph. But when they're feeding, look out. Their powerful upper tail provides sudden jolts of speed, sometimes boosting their speed to more than 20 mph when they're on the attack. And if you see one while swimming, don't turn your back. Keep your eyes on the shark and leave the water calmly.

MAKES SCENTS

The tiger shark's sense of smell is outstanding. About 60 percent of its brain is reserved for processing scents, because it sniffs out its prey. It can probably smell fear too.

HUNTING TOOLS

What else makes tiger sharks natural-born killers? Like most sharks they have a lateral line that helps them sense anything moving in the water. When the water is dark these bright sharks can feel even the smallest movements of an animal nearby. Then the hunt is on.

HOW THEY ATTACK

Tiger sharks are no kittens. They kill humans. And they like to swim where humans swim: in warm, shallow water. This dangerous species doesn't make a habit of eating people, but they'll take a bite to see what you taste like. And they'll leave quite an impression.

As with most sharks you're likelier to bleed to death from a bite than actually be eaten. But if you're already dead when one finds you, then you might be what's for dinner.

THE BIGGEST
The largest verified tiger shark was 18 feet long and 3,125 pounds. Grrr.

GREAT W

(Carcharodon carcharias)

HUMAN ATTACK RANKING

#1

NICKNAMES? Amaletz, White Death, White Pointer

HOW LONG? Usually 12 to 15 feet

HOW HEAVY? 2,500 to 3,000 pounds

MOST FAMOUS MOVIE? *Jaws*

HITE

DEATH BY TEETH

Great whites do kill people. But probably not as many as you think. There are just more than 400 recorded attacks on humans, and most of those weren't deadly. Human victims are usually swimming in murky (or dark) water where sharks mistake them for something that tastes better. Sharks probe with their mouths, and actually prefer s u r f b o a r d s to surfers.

he great white shark is the most famous deadly shark of all. No other fish has more recorded kills. No other fish strikes as much fear into the hearts of humans across the world.

You don't have to be attacked by a great white to appreciate these sharks' ferocity. They're the largest predators in the fish kingdom. For centuries great whites have been spotted at lenghs of 25 and even 30 feet. However, the average great white measures 12 to 15 feet long and generally weighs 2,500 to 3,000 pounds. The female is usually larger than the male, though both are savage beasts of prey.

HOW THEY ATTACK
If you're in shark-infested waters, don't expect to hear a movie soundtrack of piano and horns going *dun dun, dun dun, dun dun*. And don't expect to see the dorsal fin of your attacker. Great whites rarely attack head-on. They usually ambush their prey from below.

Interestingly the great white is the only shark that will lift its head above water to watch for (and smell for) its next meal. Once it fixes a victim in its beady black eyes, it swims silently downward. There it lies in wait for the shadow of its victim overhead—and then rushes upward to take a bite.

EAT OR BE EATEN
These killers are apex predators, animals at the very top of the food chain. Their only natural predators are the following mammals: orca whales, sperm whales, and of course humans.

#1 GREAT WHITE SHARK

Great white sharks prowl nearly all the cooler oceans and seas of the world. These massive predators prefer coastal waters where tasty animals swim. The highest concentration of great whites patrol the waters along South Africa.

#2 TIGER SHARK

If you're looking for tiger sharks, you should have no trouble finding them. They hunt all over the world in warm and tropical waters along every ocean coast, including harbors and estuaries. They're also found in open water, especially in the Pacific Ocean. Tigers are nomads and loners. That's OK; you don't want their company either.

#3 BULL SHARK

Because they travel in both freshwater and salt water, bull sharks really get around. They like their water tropical or temperate and they like it muddy too. (This helps them hide from their victims.) Shallow coastal waters and rivers are another haunt.

#4 SAND TIGER SHARK

These common sharks prefer shallow, sandy shores. They inhabit warm coastlines, bays, and reefs all over the world. The east coasts of the United States, southern Brazil, and Argentina are popular habitats, but interestingly, the Caribbean is not.

#5 NURSE SHARK

Adults hang out along reefs and rocky shores, remaining far below the surface—usually 200 feet or more—during the daytime. At night they move up to shallower waters 50 to 75 feet below the surface. They like things dark and quiet.

TED WATERS

#6  **SHORTFIN MAKO** The shortfin mako is a worldwide wanderer. While they prefer warm temperatures in tropical waters, they usually submerge to the cooler depths. Your odds of meeting one are pretty good: The shortfin mako is one of the most common species of shark.

#7 **BLACKTIP SHARK** Blacktip sharks don't like the open ocean. That's why they can be found on just about any warm or tropical coast in the world. Blacktips haunt oceans, bays, rivers, swamps, and more. They prefer to live at a shallow cruising depth that's less than 100 feet below the surface.

#8  **HAMMERHEAD SHARK** Great hammerheads like warm and tropical waters. Coastal areas are their favorite habitat—anywhere from the near surface to 250 feet deep. These sharks migrate, sometimes great distances, to cooler water during summer months.

#9 **BLUE SHARK** Blue sharks are pelagic, which means they don't come close to shore. They prefer to dine off shore in open waters. These frequent travelers are just about everywhere in temperate and tropical waters, but they don't like the water too hot.

#10  **LEMON SHARK** The lemon shark prefers warm coastal waters, often lurking near coral reefs, mangroves, and river mouths. It lives in the area between the surface of the water and 300 feet deep—that's the same distance as a football field.

SHARKS

- Sharks usually live 20 to 25 years, but some species can live 70 years or more.

- Sharks are always growing teeth. Some sharks can go through 30,000 teeth in their lifetime.

- Sharks are fish, fish lay eggs, and some shark species lay eggs in the water like other fish. But here's where things get interesting. In a number of shark species, it's babies and not eggs that come out of the mother shark's body. Some of these species are born after the eggs hatch inside the mother. The baby shark grows until it's ready and then enters the underwater world tail first.

- The thresher shark has the longest tail fin of any shark. Its tail fin is half of its body length.

- Sharks do not sleep. Instead they alternate between activity and rest periods.

- Most sharks are cold-blooded, which means their body temperature is the same as their environment.

- The most common shark species is the spiny dogfish shark.

- Scientists have shown that sharks can learn at a rate similar to rats and birds.

- The DC-9 airplane was modeled after the shark because engineers were looking for something that moved quickly without expending all its energy. Both have round bodies tapering off at both ends, which allows the plane to glide through the air and the shark to glide through the water.

ATISTICS

NOW YOU SEE ME NOW YOU DON'T

The camouflaged coloring of a shark—dark on top and light on the bottom—is called countershading, and enables it to blend in with its ocean environment. This works two ways: From above the dark color of the shark blends in with the dark ocean floor; from below predators looking up may not see the light underside of the shark because of the sun streaming down through the water.

BITE STRENGTH

Sharks have the most powerful jaws on the planet, which could be due to the fact that both their upper and lower jaws move.

TOP HEAVY

Sharks have asymmetrical tails; the upper half is longer than the lower half.

Sharks tend to attack humans in waters close to shore. That's where most swimmers hang out, plus sharks' favorite meals are often near shore too. Sharks get trapped at low tide along sandbars, and when that happens, be prepared for double trouble: A trapped shark is anxious and unpredictable—and it may be hungry too, by the time it meets you in the water.

An unprovoked, unexpected shark attack can follow any of the following three patterns:

1) HIT AND RUN ATTACKS

Look out, surfers. Look out, swimmers. When you're in the waves, you're in the crosshairs. And you won't see a dorsal fin cutting through the water before you're attacked. Hit and run attacks are absolutely the most common type, often the result of mistaken identity. The shark sneaks up, takes a bite, and then swims off to nearby safety. Sharks don't want conflict with their victims; they just want dinner. And since they don't particularly enjoy the taste of humans, they simply don't return after the first bite. Hit and run victims usually end up with a cut leg, some scarring, and a lifetime story to tell anyone who will listen.

2) BUMP AND BITE ATTACKS

Once swimmers, surfers, and divers move offshore, and into deep waters, they're over their heads if the bigger shark species are nearby. It's the larger sharks who specialize in bump and bite assaults, which result in greater injuries and fatalities. This style of attack begins when the shark circles its victim, moving in closer and closer to figure out the best angle of attack. Before the teeth come out, the shark bumps the victim with its head. This confuses the victim, making an attack easier.

3) SNEAK ATTACKS

The least likely attack against a human is also the most deadly. Occurring in deeper water, sneak attacks are not usually accidental tastings. With a sneak attack the shark may be hungry, but it is mainly feeling territorial or threatened by the presence of surfers, swimmers, or divers in the water. As the name implies, a sneak attack occurs without warning and the injuries are often severe or fatal.

Remember, only a few species of sharks attack humans. The great white, the tiger, and the bull are the leading human hunters. Even those species rarely go after people unprovoked. Here are some reasons sharks do turn on humans:

▶ Humans are the shark's greatest natural enemy. For every human killed each year by a shark, at least 100,000 sharks are killed. This doesn't suggest sharks seek revenge; it's just that the hunting takes place on their turf. Sharks are naturally territorial creatures. Every now and then, an incautious shark hunter ends up being the one who is hunted.

▶ If you're not hunting for shark, but you happen to be surfing or diving in a shark's personal aquarium, you may get more attention than you bargained for. Sharks guard their territory zealously.

▶ As highly evolved as sharks are, they make mistakes sometimes—mistaking humans for steaks. Humans are close in size to tasty treats like sea lions, seals, rays, big fish, and even other sharks. Sharks tend to hunt in dark, murky waters, which doesn't help them see clearly. By the time a shark finds out it's in error, your leg is in its mouth.

▶ The vast majority of shark attacks are not fatal. Even if your leg does get chomped, you don't taste so good to a shark and the leg stays put (more or less). Sharks almost never come back for a second bite.

SHARK SPREE

In 1957 the residents of Durban, South Africa earned an unfortunate title: Shark Attack Capital of the World. In less than four months (107 days), there were seven reported attacks against humans, including five fatalities.

NO HUNGER FOR HUMANS

Sorry to say, human beings aren't the appetizer of choice for sharks. Scientists believe humans are too bony, humans don't have enough fat, and/or humans simply don't taste good. Maybe this hurts human egos, but at least it's a hurt that heals.

ATTACK

GOING UP

The average number of shark attacks is rising every decade. But that's not surprising: The average number of swimmers and surfers in the water keeps getting higher too.

THE REAL DEAL

Every year 75 to 100 shark attacks are reported worldwide. Usually 10 to 15 of these attacks are fatal. The numbers are probably higher, however, since reports from underdeveloped countries are not common.

THE JERSEY SHORE ATTACKS OF 1916

Except in the movie *Jaws*—one of the scariest movies of all time—the idea of sharks terrorizing an American beach resort during the summer season almost never happens. Well, except for the shark attacks on the New Jersey shore during the first 12 days of July 1916. That was a summer of shock, horror, death, and enough excellent raw material to inspire author Peter Benchley to write the book *Jaws* on which the movie was based.

Most witnesses believe one sandbar shark caused all the mayhem. Others blame the great white and still others think the freshwater attacks could only have been perpetrated by a bull shark. But they all agree that "Seawolf," as the shark was called, killed three men and a boy in four separate attacks. In one assault a man swam out to save the boy and was himself killed. One other boy survived the last reported attack on July 12.

SHARK SAFETY TIPS

SHARK MO

GREAT WHITE

MOST WANTED

If the shark is larger than you are, chances are it's a threat. The top three most aggressive shark species are the great white shark, the tiger shark, and the bull shark. They've been identified at the scene of more crimes than any other sea creatures. Why? Their usual diet of large, human-size sea animals makes people more likely to be accidentally (or intentionally) targeted for attack.

AND IF YOU DO SEE ONE . . .

Don't turn your back. Don't splash and stay vertical. If someone else is near you, join hands, to appear larger. Back away toward land. Believe it or not, sharks can be afraid of you too.

ST WANTED

TIGER SHARK

BULL SHARK

- Swim close to shore where help is more readily available.

- Stay away from sandbars and sharp drop-offs.

- Avoid making erratic movements that attract sharks.

- If sharks are known to be around, don't swim in the area.

- If you're bleeding, it's best to stay out of the water.

- Try not to swim in the same area as where people are fishing.

- Never swim alone. Swim with buddies or in places where there are lifeguards.

- If the water is dirty or murky, don't swim.

- Sharks feed around sunset; that's a good time not to be in the water.

- Watch for fish and turtles quickly escaping the area or forming a large group. This could indicate a predator is in the area.

- Excessive splashing can attract sharks. Keep splashing to a minimum.

- Don't wear bright colors or jewelry that may look like other fish to sharks.

GLOSSARY

AMPULLAE OF LORENZINI: sensory cells that help sharks detect electric fields; this sensory organ is found around the head of a shark and used to feel the electrical field coming from its prey

ANAL FIN: fin on the lower side of a shark near the tail; not all sharks have one

BASIHYAL: a shark's tongue

BRINE SHRIMP: crustacean found in salt water

CARNIVORE: a flesh-eating animal

CAUDAL FIN: tail fin; propels shark forward

CRUSTACEAN: animals with antennae whose bodies are joined with a hardened shell

DENTICLES: small toothlike scales embedded in the skin of sharks

DORSAL FIN: fin on the upper side of the body; helps shark stabilize while swimming

GILLS: fleshy organs used for breathing; slits located on the side of the head

GILL RAKERS: located at the back of the throat, they strain tiny food from the water like a colander

LATERAL LINE: line of canals that go from head to tail; canals are filled with water and contain sensory cells with hairs growing out of them; hairs move when water vibrates and alerts shark to potential prey

NOCTURNAL: asleep during the day, awake at night

PECTORAL FIN: each of the paired fins on either side of the body, near the head (lifts the shark as it swims)

PELVIC FIN: pair of fins on the belly, behind the pectoral fins; they help control movement and provide stability

PLANKTON: tiny, floating plants and animals that live in water

SPIRACLE: small, round openings behind the eye that send water to the gills and enable some sharks to breathe while eating or resting